MARIE CURIE AND RADIOACTIVITY

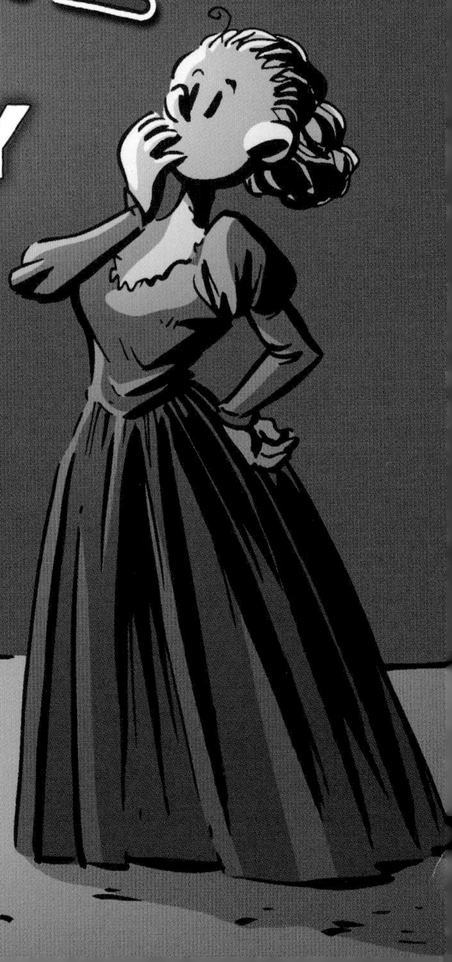

JORDI BAYARRI

GRAPHIC UNIVERSE™ • MINNEAPOLIS

Story and art by Jordi Bayarri
Coloring by Dani Seijas
Historical and scientific consultation by Dr. Tayra M. C. Lanuza-Navarro, PhD in History of Science
Translation by Patricia Ibars and John Wright

First American edition published in 2020 by Graphic Universe™

Graphic Universe™
An imprint of Lerner Publishing Group, Inc.
241 First Avenue North
Minneapolis, MN 55401 USA

For reading levels and more information, look up this title at www.lernerbooks.com.

Image credit: Bettmann/Getty Images, p. 37

Main body text set in CCDaveGibbonsLower.
Typeface provided by OpenType.

Library of Congress Cataloging-in-Publication Data

Names: Bayarri, Jordi, 1972– author, illustrator.
Title: Marie Curie and radiation / Jordi Bayarri.
Description: Minneapolis : Graphic Universe, [2020] | Series: Graphic science biographies | "Graphic Universe is a trademark of Lerner Publishing Group, Inc." | Audience: Ages 10–14. | Audience: Grades 7 to 8. | Includes bibliographical references and index.
Identifiers: LCCN 2019006971 | ISBN 9781541578210 (lb : alk. paper)
Subjects: LCSH: Curie, Marie, 1867–1934—Comic books, strips, etc. | Curie, Marie, 1867–1934—Juvenile literature. | Radioactivity—History—Comic books, strips, etc. | Radioactivity—History—Juvenile literature. | Women chemists—France—Biography—Comic books, strips, etc. | Women chemists—France—Biography—Juvenile literature. | Women Nobel Prize winners—Biography—Comic books, strips, etc. | Women Nobel Prize winners—Biography—Juvenile literature. | Discoveries in science—Comic books, strips, etc. | Discoveries in science—Juvenile literature.
Classification: LCC QD22.C8 B39 2020 | DDC 540.92 [B]—dc23

LC record available at https://lccn.loc.gov/2019006971

Manufactured in the United States of America
1-46926-47806-5/21/2019

CONTENTS

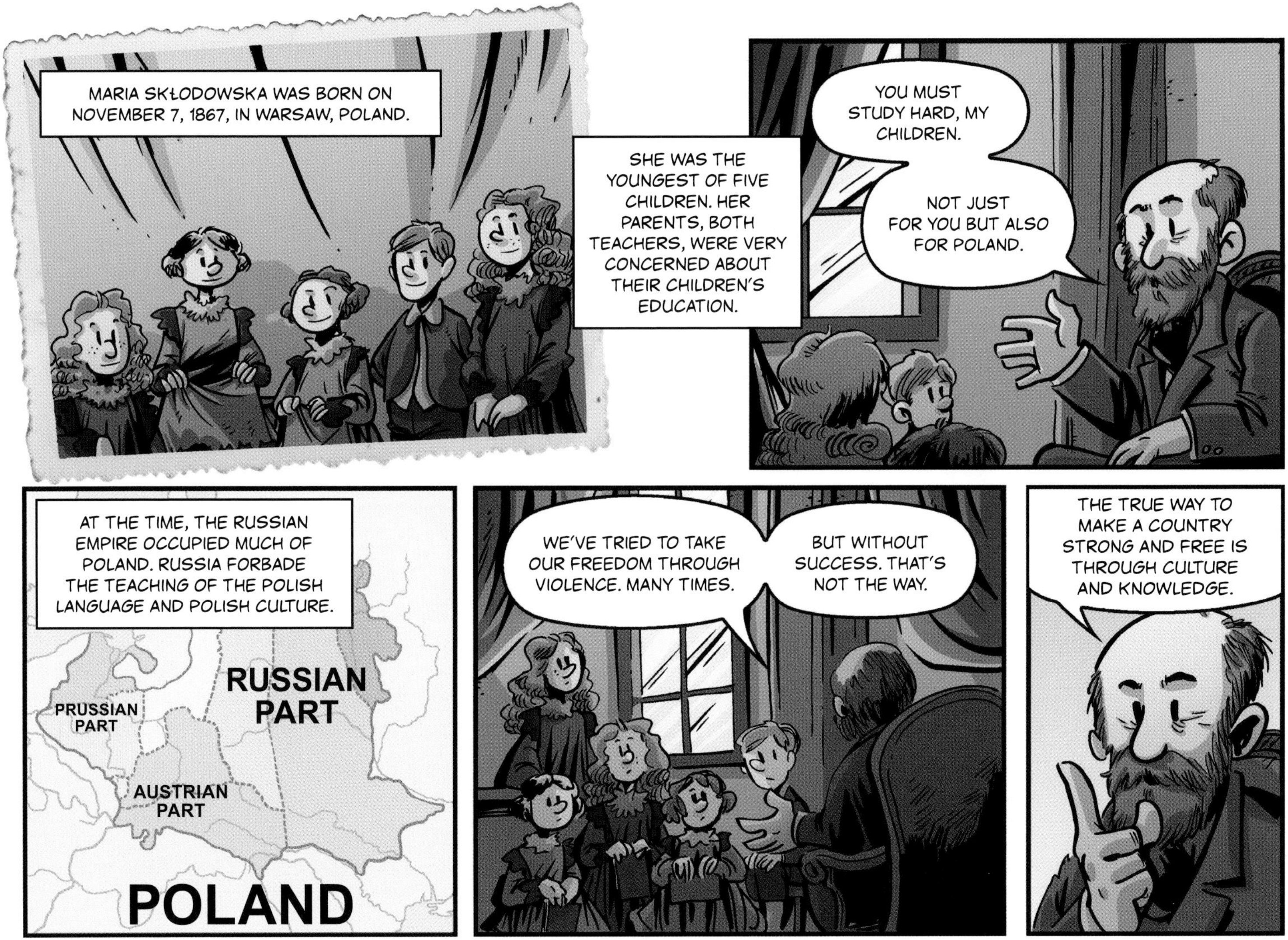

MARIA SKŁODOWSKA WAS BORN ON NOVEMBER 7, 1867, IN WARSAW, POLAND.
SHE WAS THE YOUNGEST OF FIVE CHILDREN. HER PARENTS, BOTH TEACHERS, WERE VERY CONCERNED ABOUT THEIR CHILDREN'S EDUCATION.
YOU MUST STUDY HARD, MY CHILDREN.
NOT JUST FOR YOU BUT ALSO FOR POLAND.
AT THE TIME, THE RUSSIAN EMPIRE OCCUPIED MUCH OF POLAND. RUSSIA FORBADE THE TEACHING OF THE POLISH LANGUAGE AND POLISH CULTURE.
RUSSIAN PART
PRUSSIAN PART
AUSTRIAN PART
POLAND
WE'VE TRIED TO TAKE OUR FREEDOM THROUGH VIOLENCE. MANY TIMES.
BUT WITHOUT SUCCESS. THAT'S NOT THE WAY.
THE TRUE WAY TO MAKE A COUNTRY STRONG AND FREE IS THROUGH CULTURE AND KNOWLEDGE.

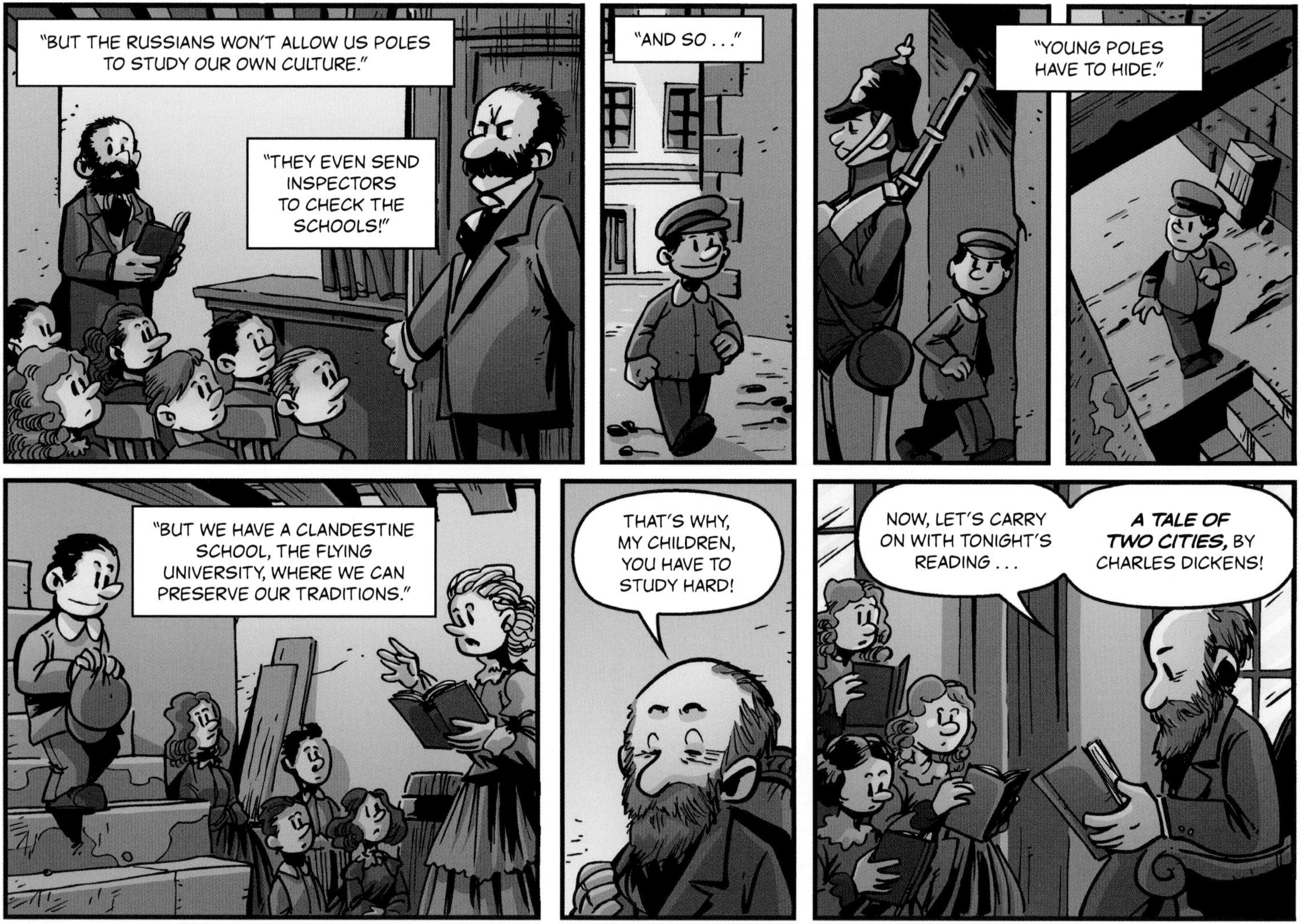
"BUT THE RUSSIANS WON'T ALLOW US POLES TO STUDY OUR OWN CULTURE."
"THEY EVEN SEND INSPECTORS TO CHECK THE SCHOOLS!"
"AND SO . . ."
"YOUNG POLES HAVE TO HIDE."
"BUT WE HAVE A CLANDESTINE SCHOOL, THE FLYING UNIVERSITY, WHERE WE CAN PRESERVE OUR TRADITIONS."
THAT'S WHY, MY CHILDREN, YOU HAVE TO STUDY HARD!
NOW, LET'S CARRY ON WITH TONIGHT'S READING . . .
A TALE OF TWO CITIES, BY CHARLES DICKENS!

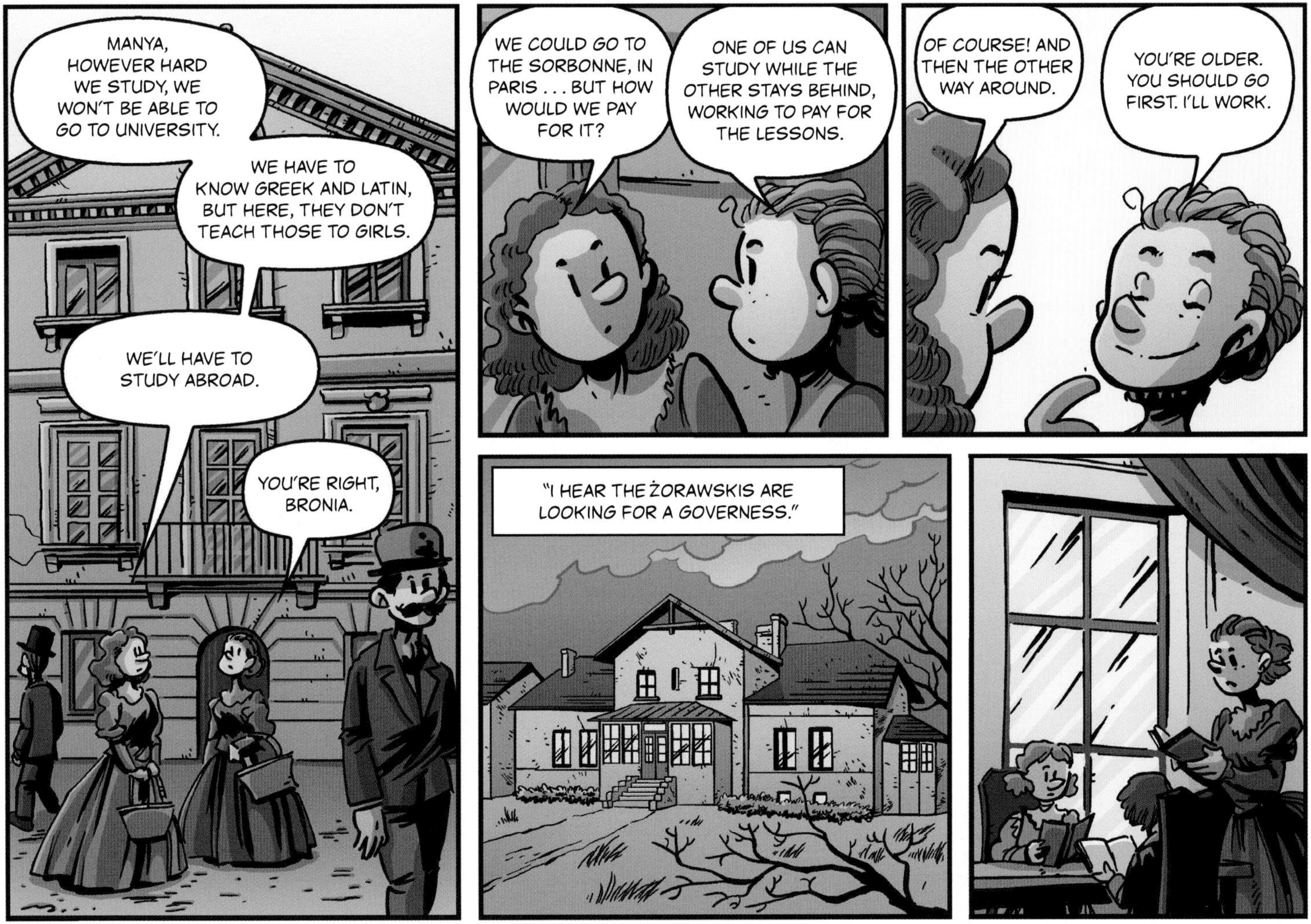
MANYA, HOWEVER HARD WE STUDY, WE WON'T BE ABLE TO GO TO UNIVERSITY.
WE HAVE TO KNOW GREEK AND LATIN, BUT HERE, THEY DON'T TEACH THOSE TO GIRLS.
WE'LL HAVE TO STUDY ABROAD.
YOU'RE RIGHT, BRONIA.
WE COULD GO TO THE SORBONNE, IN PARIS . . . BUT HOW WOULD WE PAY FOR IT?
ONE OF US CAN STUDY WHILE THE OTHER STAYS BEHIND, WORKING TO PAY FOR THE LESSONS.
OF COURSE! AND THEN THE OTHER WAY AROUND.
YOU'RE OLDER. YOU SHOULD GO FIRST. I'LL WORK.
"I HEAR THE ŻORAWSKIS ARE LOOKING FOR A GOVERNESS."

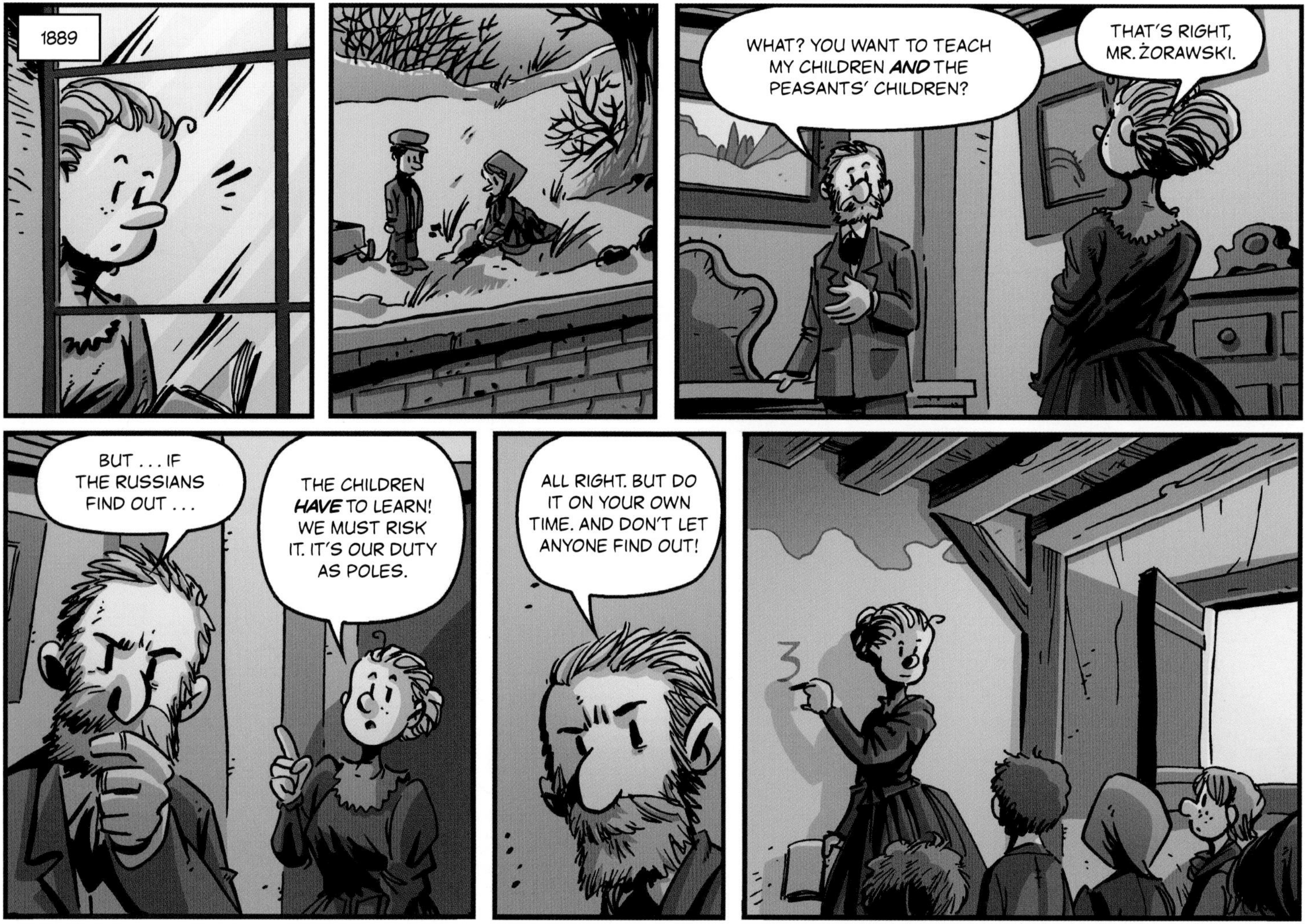
1889
WHAT? YOU WANT TO TEACH MY CHILDREN AND THE PEASANTS' CHILDREN?
THAT'S RIGHT, MR. ŻORAWSKI.
BUT . . . IF THE RUSSIANS FIND OUT . . .
THE CHILDREN HAVE TO LEARN! WE MUST RISK IT. IT'S OUR DUTY AS POLES.
ALL RIGHT. BUT DO IT ON YOUR OWN TIME. AND DON'T LET ANYONE FIND OUT!
3

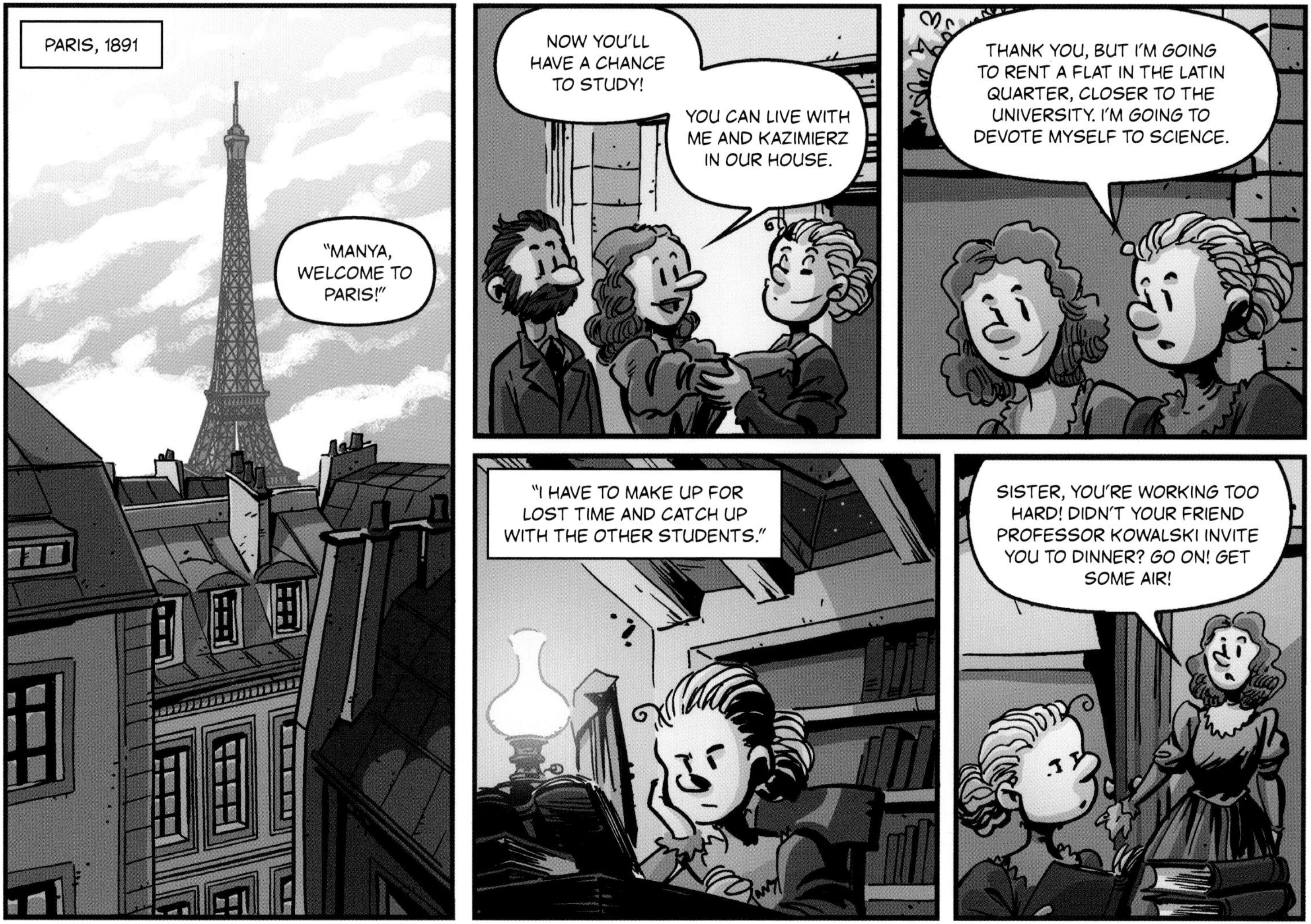
PARIS, 1891
"MANYA, WELCOME TO PARIS!"
NOW YOU'LL HAVE A CHANCE TO STUDY!
YOU CAN LIVE WITH ME AND KAZIMIERZ IN OUR HOUSE.
THANK YOU, BUT I'M GOING TO RENT A FLAT IN THE LATIN QUARTER, CLOSER TO THE UNIVERSITY. I'M GOING TO DEVOTE MYSELF TO SCIENCE.
"I HAVE TO MAKE UP FOR LOST TIME AND CATCH UP WITH THE OTHER STUDENTS."
SISTER, YOU'RE WORKING TOO HARD! DIDN'T YOUR FRIEND PROFESSOR KOWALSKI INVITE YOU TO DINNER? GO ON! GET SOME AIR!

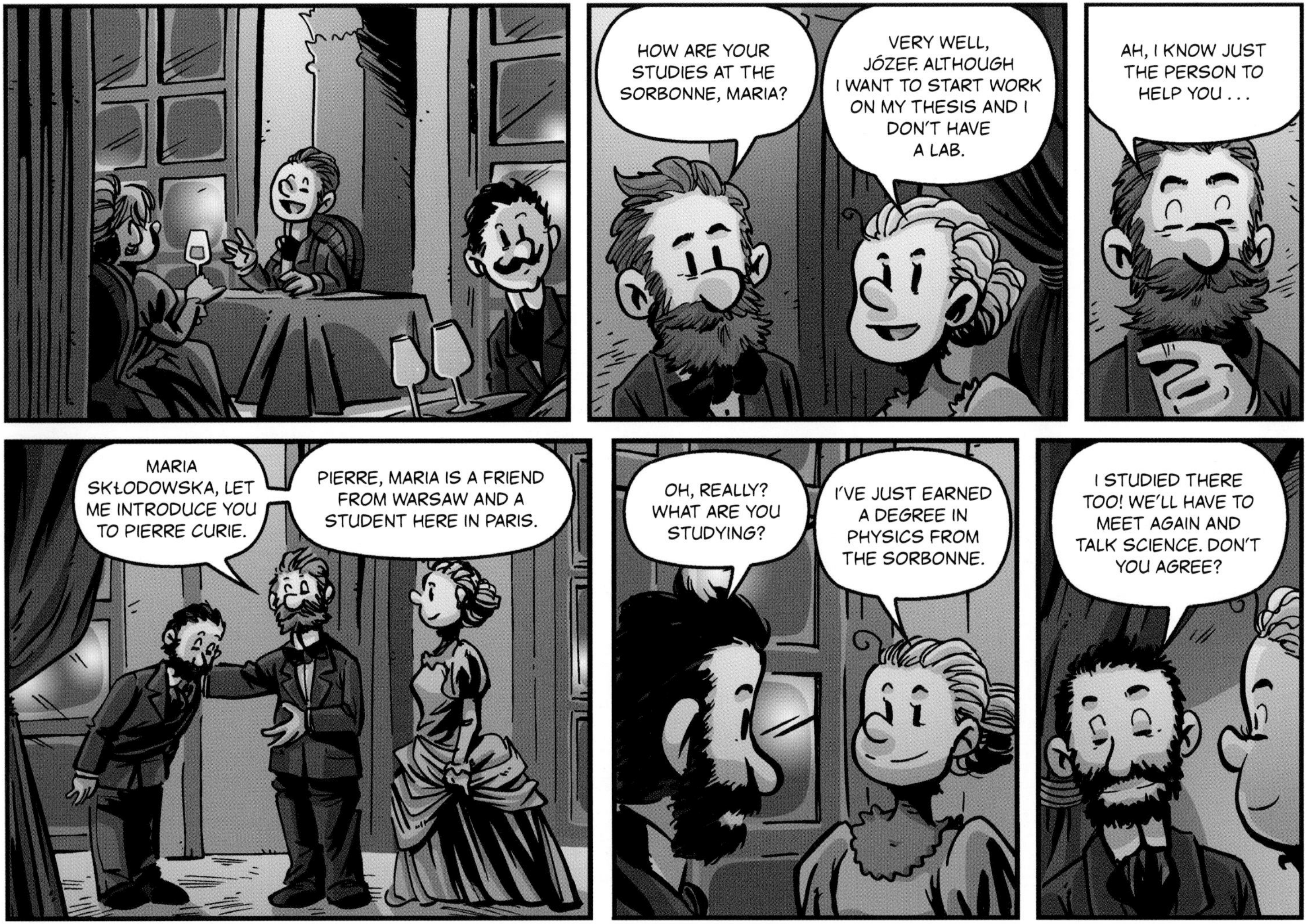
HOW ARE YOUR STUDIES AT THE SORBONNE, MARIA?
VERY WELL, JÓZEF. ALTHOUGH I WANT TO START WORK ON MY THESIS AND I DON'T HAVE A LAB.
AH, I KNOW JUST THE PERSON TO HELP YOU . . .
MARIA SKŁODOWSKA, LET ME INTRODUCE YOU TO PIERRE CURIE.
PIERRE, MARIA IS A FRIEND FROM WARSAW AND A STUDENT HERE IN PARIS.
OH, REALLY? WHAT ARE YOU STUDYING?
I'VE JUST EARNED A DEGREE IN PHYSICS FROM THE SORBONNE.
I STUDIED THERE TOO! WE'LL HAVE TO MEET AGAIN AND TALK SCIENCE. DON'T YOU AGREE?

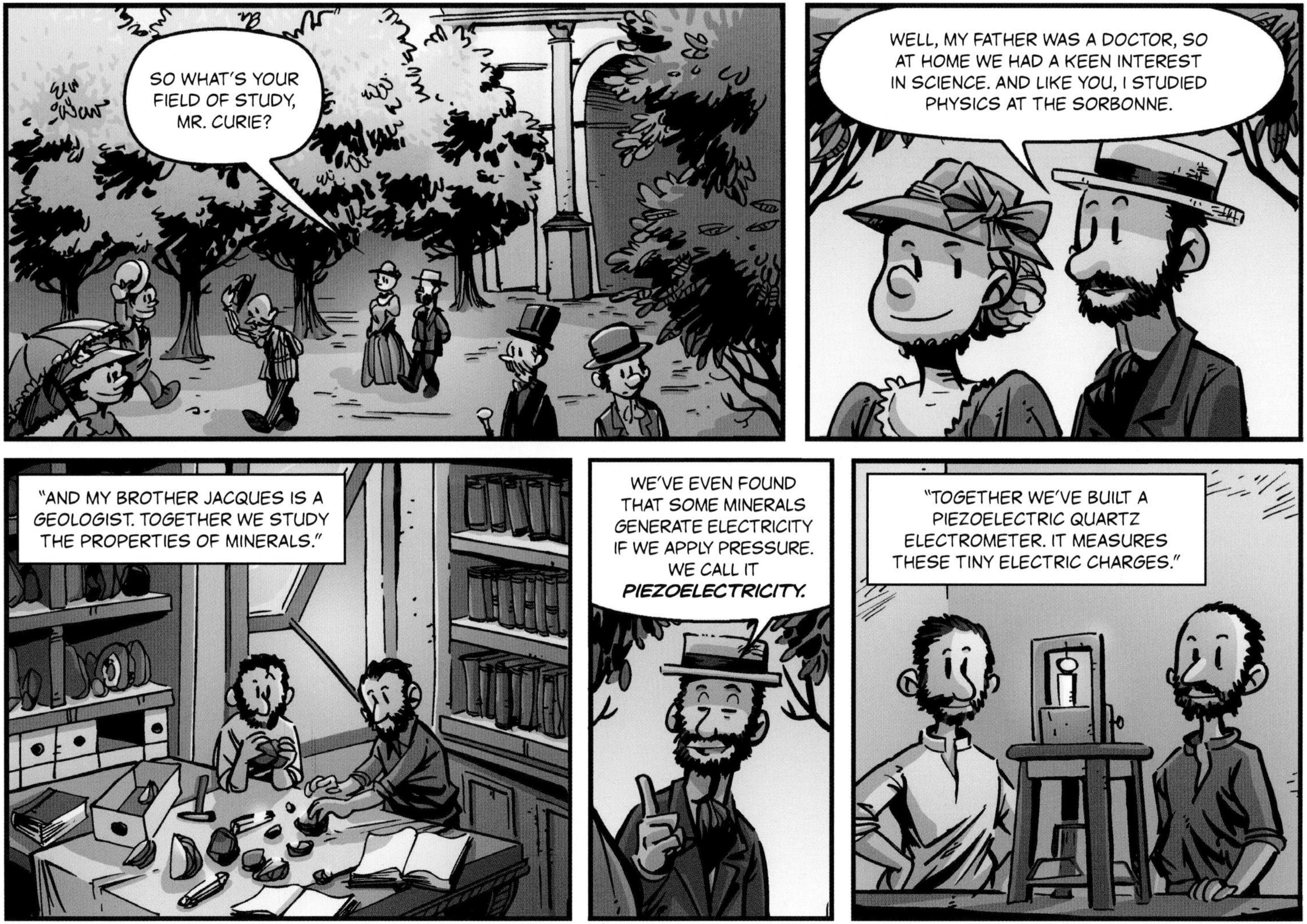
SO WHAT'S YOUR FIELD OF STUDY, MR. CURIE?
WELL, MY FATHER WAS A DOCTOR, SO AT HOME WE HAD A KEEN INTEREST IN SCIENCE. AND LIKE YOU, I STUDIED PHYSICS AT THE SORBONNE.
"AND MY BROTHER JACQUES IS A GEOLOGIST. TOGETHER WE STUDY THE PROPERTIES OF MINERALS."
WE'VE EVEN FOUND THAT SOME MINERALS GENERATE ELECTRICITY IF WE APPLY PRESSURE. WE CALL IT ***PIEZOELECTRICITY.***
"TOGETHER WE'VE BUILT A PIEZOELECTRIC QUARTZ ELECTROMETER. IT MEASURES THESE TINY ELECTRIC CHARGES."

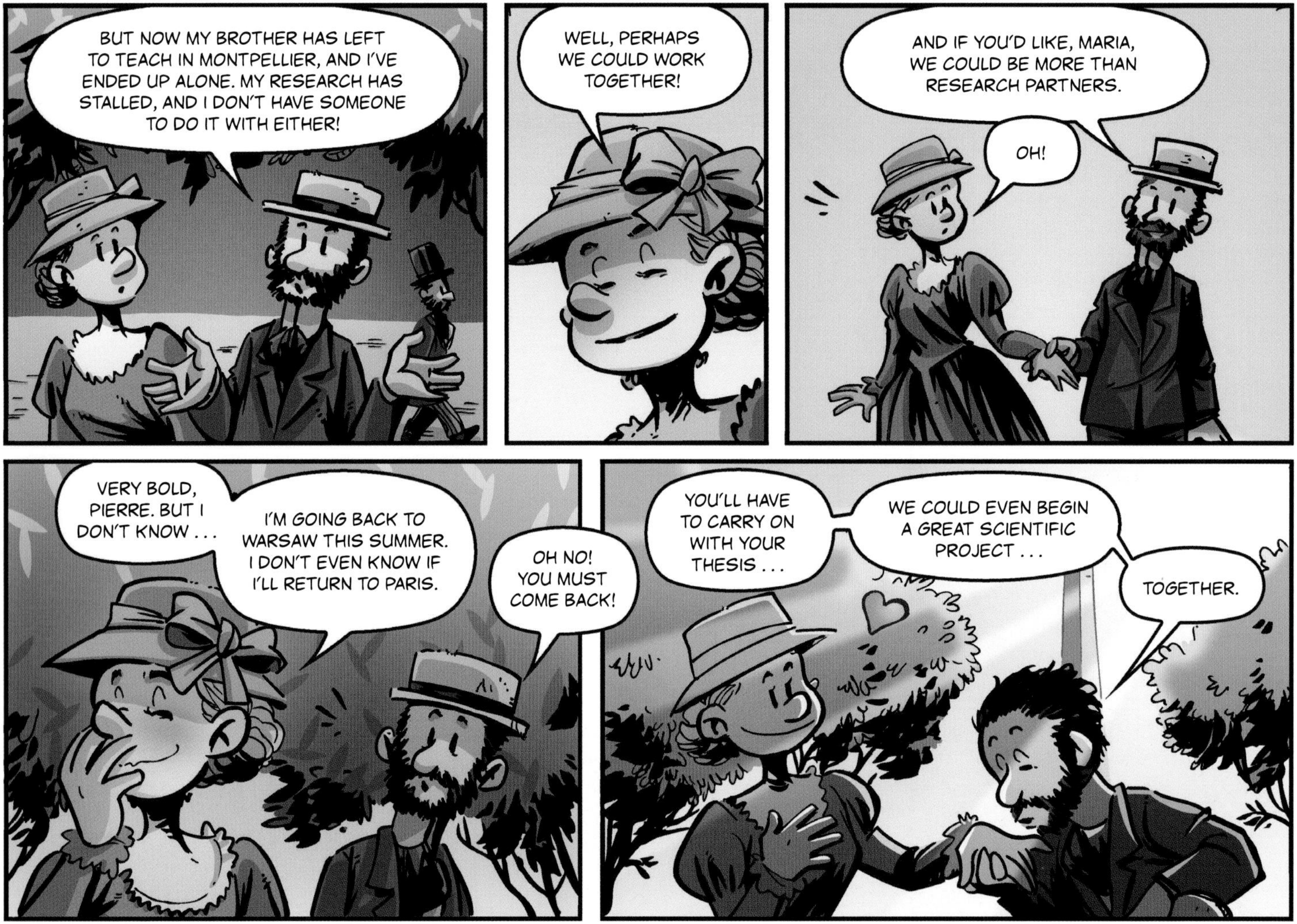
BUT NOW MY BROTHER HAS LEFT TO TEACH IN MONTPELLIER, AND I'VE ENDED UP ALONE. MY RESEARCH HAS STALLED, AND I DON'T HAVE SOMEONE TO DO IT WITH EITHER!
WELL, PERHAPS WE COULD WORK TOGETHER!
AND IF YOU'D LIKE, MARIA, WE COULD BE MORE THAN RESEARCH PARTNERS.
OH!
VERY BOLD, PIERRE. BUT I DON'T KNOW . . .
I'M GOING BACK TO WARSAW THIS SUMMER. I DON'T EVEN KNOW IF I'LL RETURN TO PARIS.
OH NO! YOU MUST COME BACK!
YOU'LL HAVE TO CARRY ON WITH YOUR THESIS . . .
WE COULD EVEN BEGIN A GREAT SCIENTIFIC PROJECT . . .
TOGETHER.

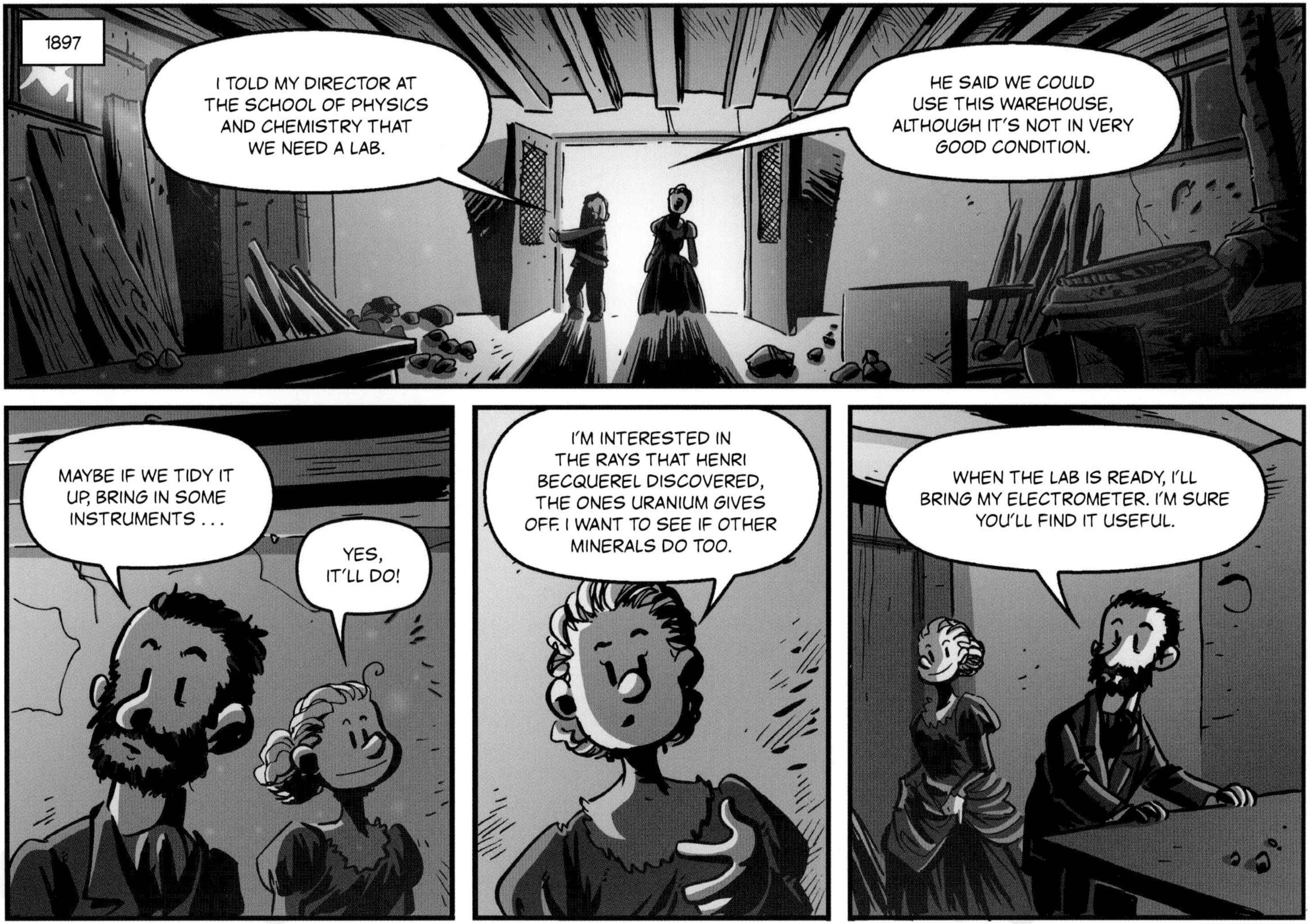
1897
I TOLD MY DIRECTOR AT THE SCHOOL OF PHYSICS AND CHEMISTRY THAT WE NEED A LAB.
HE SAID WE COULD USE THIS WAREHOUSE, ALTHOUGH IT'S NOT IN VERY GOOD CONDITION.
MAYBE IF WE TIDY IT UP, BRING IN SOME INSTRUMENTS . . .
YES, IT'LL DO!
I'M INTERESTED IN THE RAYS THAT HENRI BECQUEREL DISCOVERED, THE ONES URANIUM GIVES OFF. I WANT TO SEE IF OTHER MINERALS DO TOO.
WHEN THE LAB IS READY, I'LL BRING MY ELECTROMETER. I'M SURE YOU'LL FIND IT USEFUL.

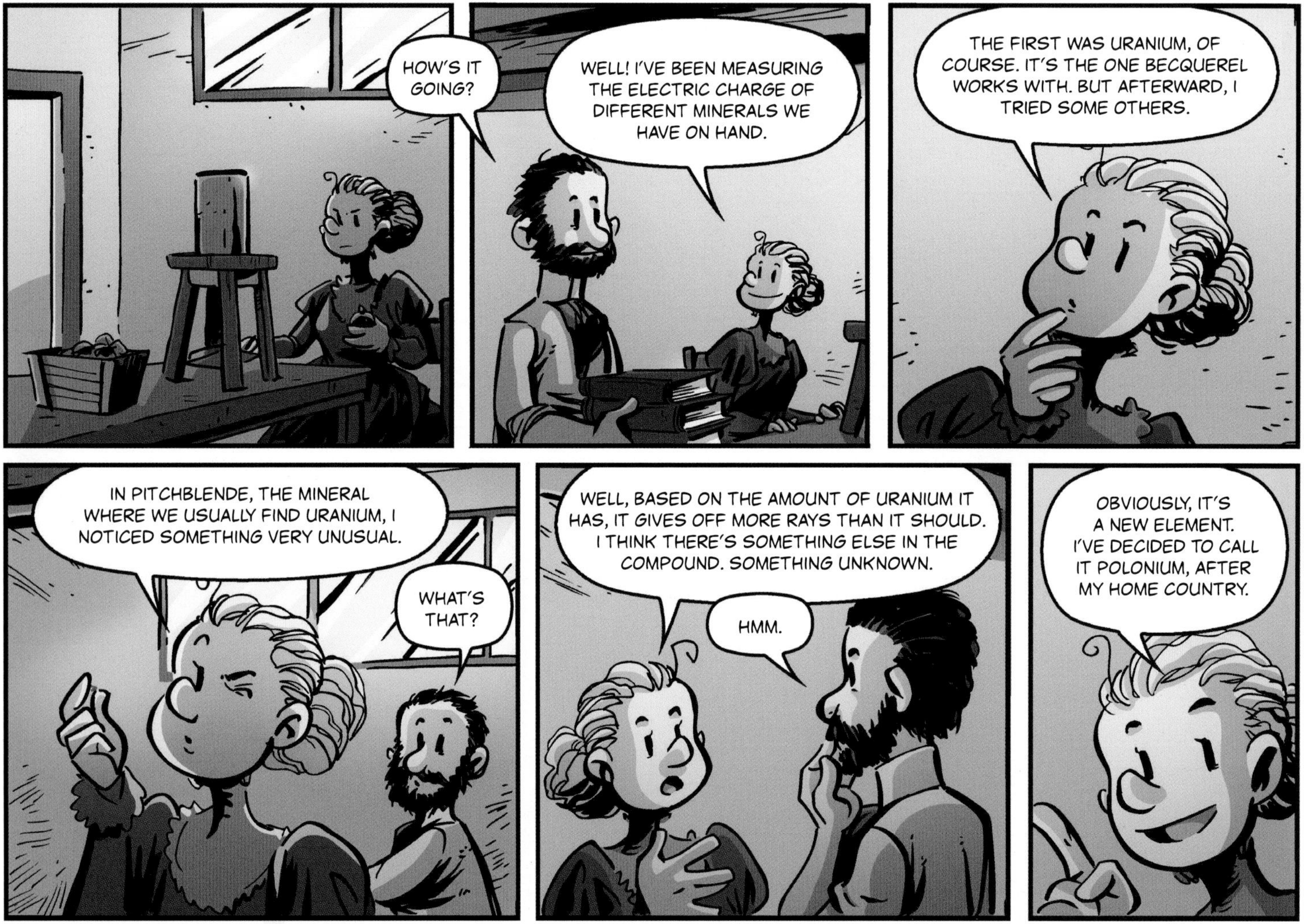
HOW'S IT GOING?
WELL! I'VE BEEN MEASURING THE ELECTRIC CHARGE OF DIFFERENT MINERALS WE HAVE ON HAND.
THE FIRST WAS URANIUM, OF COURSE. IT'S THE ONE BECQUEREL WORKS WITH. BUT AFTERWARD, I TRIED SOME OTHERS.
IN PITCHBLENDE, THE MINERAL WHERE WE USUALLY FIND URANIUM, I NOTICED SOMETHING VERY UNUSUAL.
WHAT'S THAT?
WELL, BASED ON THE AMOUNT OF URANIUM IT HAS, IT GIVES OFF MORE RAYS THAN IT SHOULD. I THINK THERE'S SOMETHING ELSE IN THE COMPOUND. SOMETHING UNKNOWN.
HMM.
OBVIOUSLY, IT'S A NEW ELEMENT. I'VE DECIDED TO CALL IT POLONIUM, AFTER MY HOME COUNTRY.

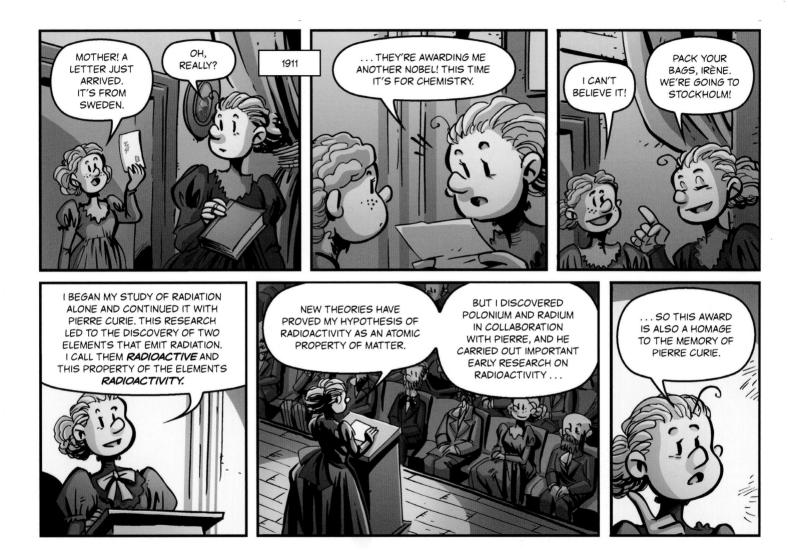

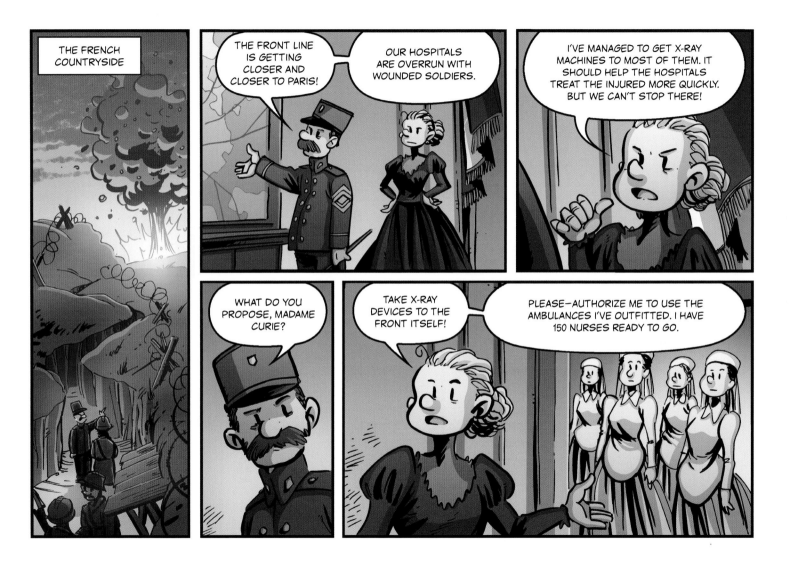

THE FRENCH COUNTRYSIDE

THE FRONT LINE IS GETTING CLOSER AND CLOSER TO PARIS!

OUR HOSPITALS ARE OVERRUN WITH WOUNDED SOLDIERS.

I'VE MANAGED TO GET X-RAY MACHINES TO MOST OF THEM. IT SHOULD HELP THE HOSPITALS TREAT THE INJURED MORE QUICKLY. BUT WE CAN'T STOP THERE!

WHAT DO YOU PROPOSE, MADAME CURIE?

TAKE X-RAY DEVICES TO THE FRONT ITSELF!

PLEASE—AUTHORIZE ME TO USE THE AMBULANCES I'VE OUTFITTED. I HAVE 150 NURSES READY TO GO.

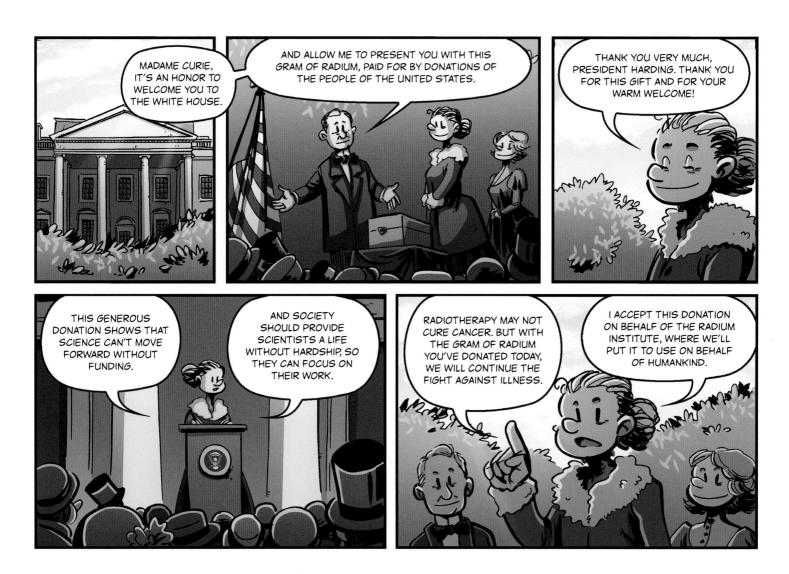

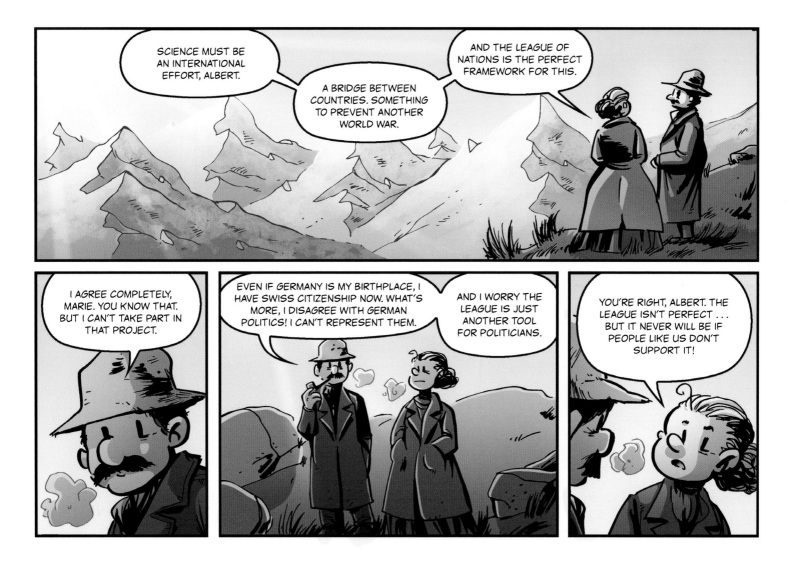

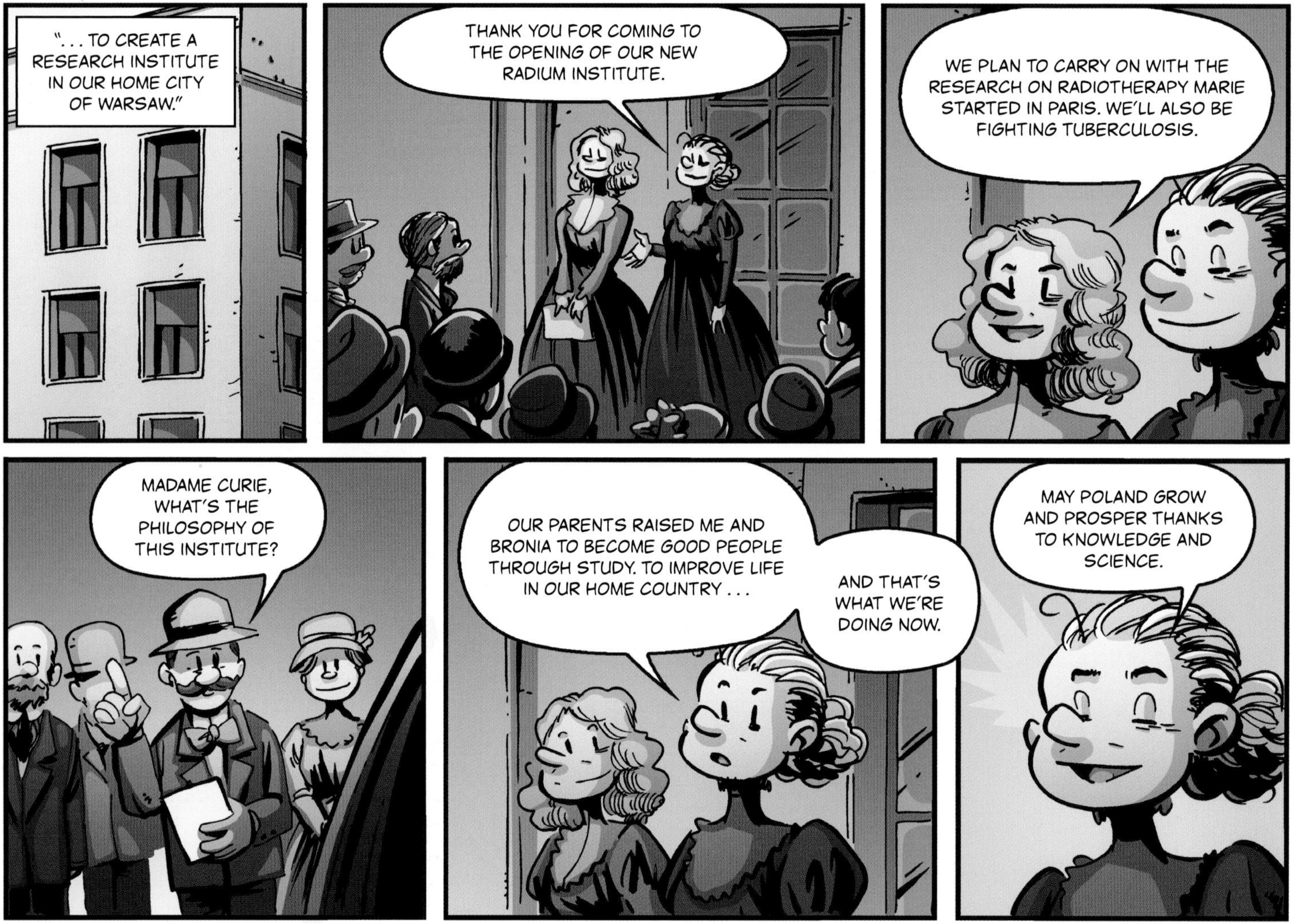
". . . TO CREATE A RESEARCH INSTITUTE IN OUR HOME CITY OF WARSAW."
THANK YOU FOR COMING TO THE OPENING OF OUR NEW RADIUM INSTITUTE.
WE PLAN TO CARRY ON WITH THE RESEARCH ON RADIOTHERAPY MARIE STARTED IN PARIS. WE'LL ALSO BE FIGHTING TUBERCULOSIS.
MADAME CURIE, WHAT'S THE PHILOSOPHY OF THIS INSTITUTE?
OUR PARENTS RAISED ME AND BRONIA TO BECOME GOOD PEOPLE THROUGH STUDY. TO IMPROVE LIFE IN OUR HOME COUNTRY . . .
AND THAT'S WHAT WE'RE DOING NOW.
MAY POLAND GROW AND PROSPER THANKS TO KNOWLEDGE AND SCIENCE.

TIMELINE

1867 Maria Salomea Skłodowska (often called Manya) is born in Warsaw, Poland, on November 7.

1873 Her father, Władysław Skłodowski, loses his position as a teacher in Russian-controlled Poland because of his pro-Polish views.

1891 Maria Skłodowska begins her studies at the University of Paris in Paris, France. She soon begins to use the name Marie.

1895 She marries Pierre Curie on July 26.

1898 Marie and Pierre Curie announce the discoveries of polonium in July and radium in December.

1903 Marie and Pierre Curie receive the Nobel Prize in Physics.

1906 Pierre Curie dies on April 19.

1911 Marie Curie wins the Nobel Prize in Chemistry.

1914 World War I begins.

1921 Curie tours the United States and receives a gram of radium from US president Warren G. Harding.

1934 She dies on July 4 from aplastic anemia.

GLOSSARY

CLANDESTINE: done in secret

ELECTRIC CHARGE: the amount of electricity held by a body, based on its balance of protons and electrons

ELECTROMETER: a device that measures electric charge

EMISSION: the act of sending out something such as energy or gas

FRONT: an area where military forces are fighting

GOVERNESS: a woman who is paid to care for and teach a child in the child's house

HYPOTHESIS: an unproven idea that leads to further study

MINERAL: a substance that is naturally formed under the ground

OCCUPIED: controlled by foreign soldiers or a foreign government

PITCHBLENDE: a mineral that contains radium and is the main ore-mineral source of uranium

QUANTUM PHYSICS: a branch of physics focused on very small particles

RADIOACTIVITY: having or producing a powerful form of energy called radiation

RAY: a thin beam of energy that moves as waves

RENOUNCE: to refuse or give up

SHRAPNEL: small pieces of metal that shoot outward from an exploding bomb, shell, or mine

SORBONNE: a public research university in Paris, France

THESIS: a long piece of writing that a researcher creates to earn a degree at a university

X-RAY: a powerful, invisible ray that can pass through various objects and make it possible to see inside some of them

FURTHER RESOURCES

Barr, Briony, Jeremy Barr, Gregory Crocetti, Ben Hutchings, and Ailsa Wild. *The Invisible War: A World War I Tale on Two Scales.* Minneapolis: Graphic Universe, 2019.

Bayarri, Jordi. *Albert Einstein and the Theory of Relativity.* Minneapolis: Graphic Universe, 2020.

Famous Scientists: Marie Curie
    https://www.famousscientists.org/marie-curie

"The Genius of Marie Curie"
    https://youtu.be/w6JFRi0Qm_s

Leigh, Anna. *30-Minute Chemistry Projects.* Minneapolis: Lerner Publications, 2019.

Marsico, Katie. *Key Discoveries in Physical Science.* Minneapolis: Lerner Publications, 2015.

INDEX